This is the Book of the Dead of Hunefer.
It is 39 cm tall and 5.5 m long.

Hunefer
and his
Book
of the
Dead

Richard Parkinson

THE BRITISH MUSEUM PRESS

For George Robinson and Gabriel Walsh.
And also for Carolyn Jones, an ideal editor, colleague and friend.

AUTHOR'S NOTE
My thanks are due to Bridget Leach for examining the papyrus with me;
Gabriel Walsh for reading a draft; John Taylor; Carolyn Jones;
Coralie Hepburn; and Nadine Cherpion for help with Inherkhau.

The Papyrus of Hunefer is now in the British Museum and its inventory number is EA 9901.
It is 39 cm tall and 5.5 metres long. It was cut into eight sheets in modern times.

© 2010 Richard Parkinson

First published in 2010 by
The British Museum Press
A division of The British Museum Company Ltd
38 Russell Square, London WC1B 3QQ
www.britishmuseum.org

Richard Parkinson has asserted his right to be identified as the author of this work.

ISBN 978 0 7141 3142 9

A catalogue record is available from the British Library

Designed by Price Watkins
Printed in China by SC (Sang Choy) International H.K. Limited

ILLUSTRATIONS
All illustrations © The Trustees of the British Museum, except pp. 5, 7 (above right), 14, 26 (centre) (R.B. Parkinson);
pp. 6–7 (IFAO, J.F. Gout); p. 37 (De Agostini / SuperStock); back endpaper (Hemis.fr / SuperStock). British Museum inventory
numbers: papyrus of Hunefer, EA 9901; unrolled papyrus, p. 8, EA 10748; papyrus of Ani, pp. 8–9, 36, EA 10470; pillar amulet, p. 15,
EA 20623; heart amulet, p. 23, EA 15619; canopic jars, p. 33, EA 59197; Osiris figure, p. 38, EA 9861.

The papers used in this book are natural and recyclable products and the manufacturing processes are
expected to conform to the environmental regulations of the country of origin.

Contents

Hunefer and his book of spells

This is a book about an Ancient Egyptian book. It was owned by a man called Hunefer, who lived in Egypt over three thousand years ago (around 1280 BC). He was in charge of the farms and cattle of the great king Menmaatre Sety I. His job titles included 'the Steward of the King, the Lord of Egypt Menmaatre', 'Overseer of the Cattle of the Lord of Egypt' and 'the Royal Scribe (secretary) in the west of Thebes', today's Luxor.

Hunefer's wife was called Nasha, and she was a priestess in the great temple of Amun at Thebes. Here they are, dressed in their best clothes and jewellery. Nasha holds a

bouquet of papyrus and the musical instrument that she used in the temple.

When Hunefer died, he was buried with a book of spells that he hoped would let him live after death. This 'Book of the Dead' has survived with his name and titles, and that is all that we know about him. We don't even know exactly where he was buried – only that he once owned this beautiful papyrus book.

Above: The funerary temple of Sety I on the west bank at Thebes. It was once surrounded by offices and storerooms. Hunefer may have worked here.

Left: Hunefer's name means 'Happy Day' in Ancient Egyptian. This is his name in hieroglyphs. You can find it written on almost every part of the papyrus.

Avoiding the dangers of death

The Egyptians loved life and hated death. They did everything they could to stay alive for ever, and like many other people, they had complex beliefs about life after death. Their funerals were very elaborate. This 'Book of the Dead' was one of their ways to try to defeat death.

But Hunefer was probably not sure that his book of spells would work. The Egyptians knew that death is not such an easy enemy to defeat, and that everyone has to die. Tombs were meant to protect the dead and keep them alive, but the Egyptians saw that even the tombs of famous princes had fallen into ruin.

Hunefer probably heard a well-known harpist's song that advised people to enjoy life while they could, and to 'spend a happy day' just like his name, 'Happy Day'.

This painting is in the tomb of an artist called Inherkhau. It shows a harpist singing his song to Inherkhau and his wife.

The tomb of the famous prince Hordedef was already ruined when Hunefer was alive. Egyptians told stories about unhappy ghosts who wandered the earth because their tombs were ruined and their names forgotten.

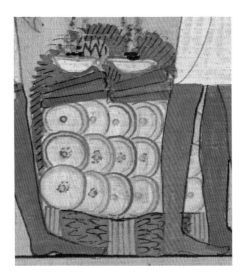

Offerings of food and water were made in tombs for the dead.

'Spells for coming forth by day'

The 'Book of the Dead' is a modern name given to what the ancient Egyptians called the 'Spells for coming forth by day'. This was a huge collection of spells which would turn a dead person into a spirit who could stay alive and emerge from the tomb into the daylight, like the rising sun.

At the time Hunefer lived, each person's book had a selection of these spells. How many you had depended on how big a book you could afford.

Knowing some of the spells, or even just owning a book of them, would give you powers to overcome danger. There were many dangers that might stop you from moving successfully between the land of the living and the land of the dead.

This is a papyrus book of spells, rolled up. It has never been opened.

These are spells from a papyrus owned by another scribe, called Ani. Some are spells for amulets, others for being able to breathe (Ani is carrying a sail to indicate air) or for allowing you water to drink (Ani and his wife are seen in a stream).

So there are spells for many different things that might happen on your journey into the land of the dead. They do not form a step-by-step story of the journey. Instead, they give you help, such as 'letting you breathe in the land of the dead' or 'turning yourself into any shape you want'.

There are spells for escaping from demons, spells for amulets, spells 'for making you remembered in the land of the dead', 'for not having your head cut off in the land of the dead' and 'for ascending into the sky'. With these spells, Hunefer will become like one of the gods, the 'lords of eternity'.

How to read a papyrus

Hunefer's book is very different from a modern book. It is a long roll of papyrus, which is an ancient sort of paper made from reeds. To read this book, you unroll it from its left end.

Books of spells like this were made in workshops, following ancient traditions. First, painters painted the pictures, and then the copyists copied out the text into the spaces around them.

Hunefer's spells were written on a roll of fine new papyrus, 39 cm tall. It must have been very expensive. Hunefer's pictures are lavish and beautifully drawn, and they were probably the most important thing. The writing is rushed, with some mistakes. Probably no one ever read this book: it was just written to be buried with its owner. The text is written in hieroglyphs in vertical lines. To read it, you start from the top left and read down the first line to the bottom, and then move right to the next line, and so on.

These books of spells were usually ready-made, with gaps left for the owner's name. When Hunefer bought this papyrus, another copyist wrote in his name and titles in slightly different handwriting.

The copyists who copied out the text used red ink for important words such as the title of a spell. It is rather like how we use *italic letters* in modern books.

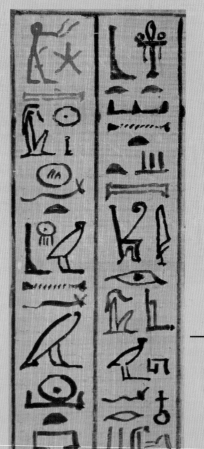

Hunefer's name

Each picture has a yellow strip around it. The same yellow strips mark the end of spells.

The start: sunrise and rebirth

The book begins with a hymn, called '*Worshipping* the Sun god when he rises in the eastern horizon of the sky'. The first thing we see is Hunefer and his wife, with their arms raised as they worship the dawn.

The hymn poetically describes the sun as:

'the creator of people and cattle,
maker of heaven and earth …
You look over millions of lands!'

It ends:

'Hail sun disk, lord of rays! When you rise everyone lives. Let me see you at the dawn of every day!'

To the left is a short blank margin to stop the start of the book getting ragged. Unfortunately, this did not work completely.

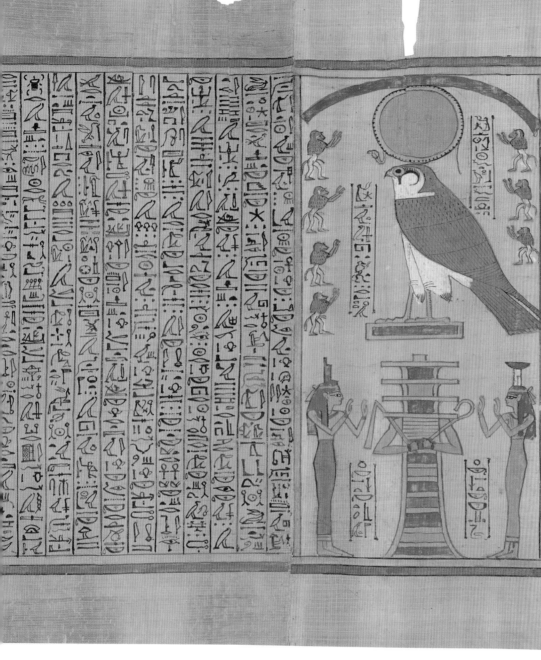

⌄ Here there is a join: the copyist found that the illustrator had left him too much space for this hymn, so he cut a bit out of the roll and shortened it!

Hunefer speaks this hymn because he hopes to be reborn, just like the sun. Each night the Sun god sets in the west and then rises again triumphantly the next morning in 'the eastern horizon'. Hunefer will do the same.

The sun rising above modern Luxor (ancient Thebes).

The illustration shows gods acting out the dawn. At the bottom Osiris, the god of the dead, is worshipped by his two sisters. He is shown as a pillar with arms holding royal sceptres. Osiris ruled the West, which was the land of the dead.

Above him stands the Sun god in the form of a hawk. Baboons are adoring him. These animals chatter loudly each dawn and so they are shown as worshipping the sun. The Sun god is about to fly into the sky, eternally shining and alive.

An amulet in the shape of the pillar of Osiris. You can see the picture and spell for this amulet on p.8.

Into the kingdom of the dead

Hunefer and his wife now worship the god of the dead, Osiris, with another hymn. This hymn is rather special — it is not found in many other papyri. Hunefer says:

> 'I have come to you,
> O son of the Sky-goddess,
> Osiris, ruler of all time!
> I am in the following
> of Thoth, and I rejoice
> at what he has done'.

He says this because Thoth once helped Osiris. And then he asks Osiris to:

> 'let me be in the following of your Majesty, just as I was on earth ... I have not done any evil in this land.'

In the labels to this picture, the careless copyist who added the owners' names onto the papyrus accidentally gave Nasha her husband's name instead of her own!

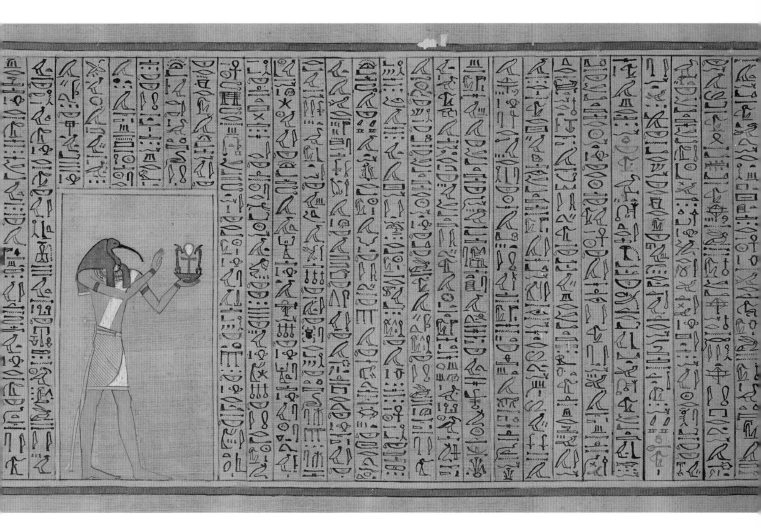

The ibis-headed god
Thoth also worships Osiris.

This yellow strip should mark the
end of the spell, but it is in the middle
of the hymn – another mistake.

Thoth and Osiris

I n this hymn to Osiris, Hunefer identifies himself with the god Thoth. Thoth was the scribe (secretary) of the gods. Hunefer says:

> '*I am* Thoth, the clever
> scribe, with clean hands ...
> who drives away evil,
> who writes truth ...
> *I am* Thoth, the lord of
> truth, who helps the poor.'

Because Thoth was the secretary of Osiris, he is an especially good person to help Hunefer, who is a secretary like him, to enter the afterlife.
Osiris was a god who ruled

Thoth worships Osiris and presents him with signs for 'power' and 'life'.

Egypt near the start of time, but his wicked brother killed him. His wife Isis mummified him and brought him back to life with Thoth's help.

There was a great court case and the gods judged that Osiris had been good and that his son Horus should rule as his heir. And so every dead Egyptian hoped to be mummified and to be given eternal life like Osiris. This is why in these spells the dead person is always called 'the Osiris X'.

Osiris became the king of the underworld and the judge of the dead. This is why Hunefer asks Osiris to be his king.

Hunefer, Nasha and Thoth stand facing the figure of Osiris in the next picture, which shows how Hunefer is judged by the gods.

Judged by the gods

This detailed picture shows how the gods will judge Hunefer after he has died. It shows three episodes. If he passes this test, he will enter the Afterlife and live for ever.

1 Anubis, the jackal-headed god of embalming, leads Hunefer into the great hall of judgement in the land of the dead, watched by the gods.

2 Hunefer's heart is weighed in a set of scales to see if he has led a good life. Thoth, the secretary of the gods, records the verdict. He says 'Look, I am recording the name of the Osiris, the Royal Scribe Hunefer. His heart has come from the scales and hasn't been found faulty'.

3 Then Horus, the son of Osiris, leads Hunefer to his father, and says 'Look, I am introducing to you the Osiris Hunefer, true of voice. He has been judged by the scales.' 'True of voice' means that the gods believe Hunefer when he claims to have led a good life.

In the hall, on a throne under a great gold canopy, just like a king, sits 'Osiris, greatest of the Westerners (the dead)'. His wife and his sister attend on him.

Under the scales sits a monster called 'Eater of the Dead', who will swallow anyone whose heart fails the test. She is watching to see if Thoth will let her eat Hunefer's heart and she has turned back to look at him.

She is made up of different frightening animals. The text above her says:

'Her front is a crocodile's,
her backside is a hippopotamus's
and her middle is a lion's.'

The god Anubis checks that the scales are balancing correctly.

Hunefer's heart is weighed against a feather, which is a sign that writes the ancient Egyptian word *Maat*. *Maat* means 'truth', but also 'justice', 'order', 'right' – everything that was valued in ancient Egypt.

Above the scales, the copyist wrote a 'spell of the heart' that tells Hunefer's own heart not to betray him:

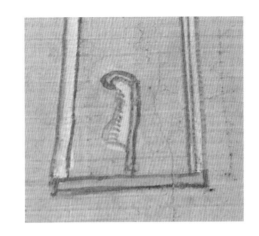

'Do not stand against me as a witness, do not oppose me in the court! Do not make my name stink in front of the great god, lord of the West (Osiris)!'

This important spell was often carved onto stone amulets of the heart like this one. Heart amulets were placed on mummies to help them pass the test.

A spell for the day of burial

At the back of the procession is a chest containing the organs of the body removed in mummification. Then Hunefer's mummy is pulled by men and cattle on a sledge shaped like a boat.

The hymns and the picture of the judgement are a sort of introduction. Now the book of spells really starts. This first spell is *'to be recited on the day of burial'* and so the illustration shows the procession to Hunefer's tomb, and his funeral.

In this spell Hunefer speaks as if he were the god Thoth to Osiris 'the king of eternity'. He also gives orders to some other gods to let him safely through:

> '*O* you who open roads ...
> for good souls in the realm of
> Osiris, open a road ... for the
> soul of the Steward Hunefer!'

After this comes a short *'spell to give a mouth to'* Hunefer. This spell is part of the funeral ceremony, which you can see on the next pages.

A man carries some of
Hunefer's belongings – a
chair and a pen box – to be
put into his burial chamber
beside his mummy.

A group of weeping
women. At the front
of the procession is
a priest reciting spells
from a papyrus roll.

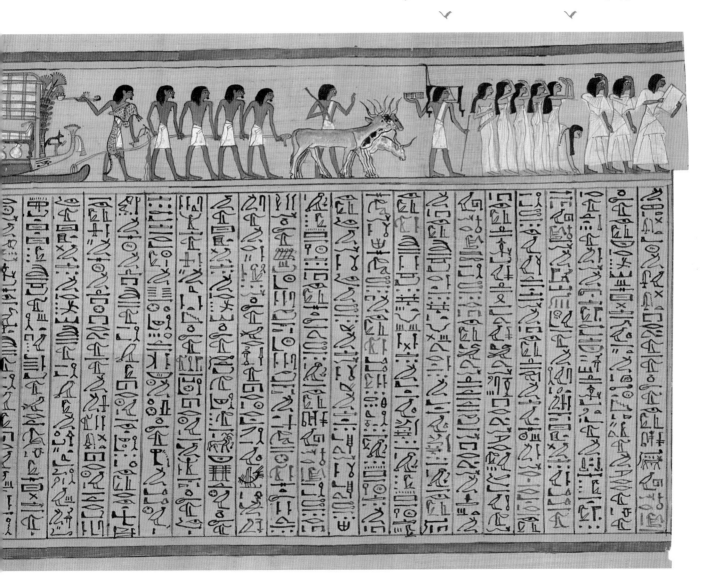

The procession ends with a detailed picture showing the final act of the funeral. This takes place at the door of the tomb-chapel above the hidden chamber where Hunefer will be buried. The god of mummification, Anubis, holds Hunefer's mummy, and Nasha weeps. The priests do their work to bring about his rebirth. They use carpentry tools to symbolically open the mouth of the mummy, so that Hunefer will be able to breathe and speak again.

Above the scene are written the words the priests have to say as they open the mummy's mouth:

'You are pure just like Horus is pure, and vice-versa …'

Hunefer's tomb-chapel is a small white building with a miniature pyramid on top, like this one near Thebes, modern Luxor.

Right: At the bottom there is a table of priestly equipment. Men have cut off the leg of a little calf to offer to the mummy as food.

A spell of questions and answers

A yellow strip shows that a new spell starts here. This spell is about:

'going out of and coming into the land of the dead, being a spirit in the lovely West, coming forth by day, changing shape into any shape that he wants, *playing board games sitting in a pavilion, coming forth as a living soul ... after he has died'.*

In this spell Hunefer says that he knows many things about the world of the gods, but he is tested about each of them. The spell gives him the right answers.

Hunefer says:

'I know yesterday;
I know tomorrow'
'What does that mean?'
'As for "yesterday",
that is Osiris. As for
"tomorrow", that is
the Sun god'.

In other words, Hunefer knows and controls all time. The past and the future are represented by two gods, Osiris and the Sun god. They are the gods Hunefer has worshipped in the hymns earlier in the papyrus. A picture shows these gods as two lions who guard the horizon where the sun rises.

Hunefer comes and goes away from the symbol of the West.

Hunefer enjoying himself
'playing board games'.

His 'living soul' is shown
as a human-headed bird.

Hunefer worships the lions
of yesterday and tomorrow.

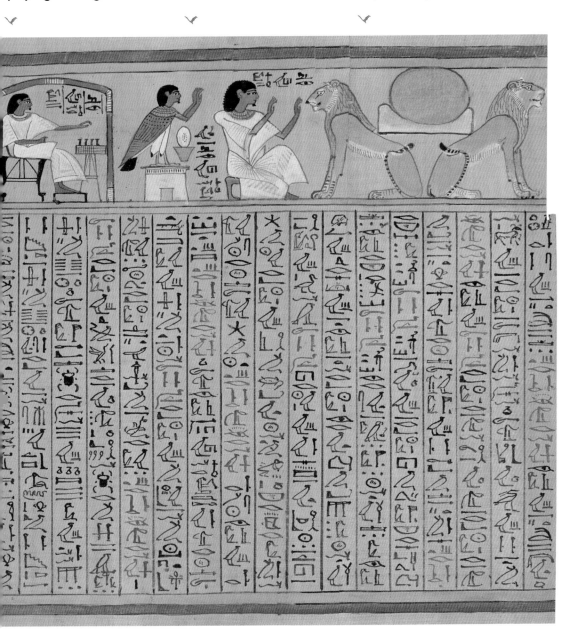

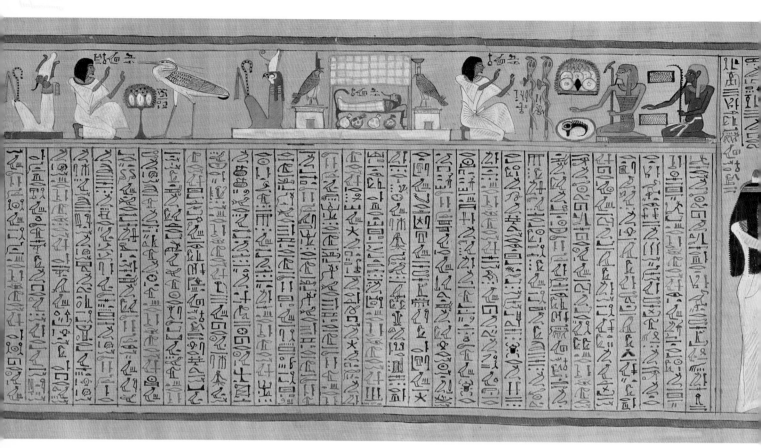

The pictures show some more of the
gods who are talked about in the spell.

This long spell of questions and answers
was a very important one and had been
used in funerals for many centuries.
With all its questions and answers, it
gives Hunefer knowledge that will let
him become like the gods. This spell
was considered to be very mysterious

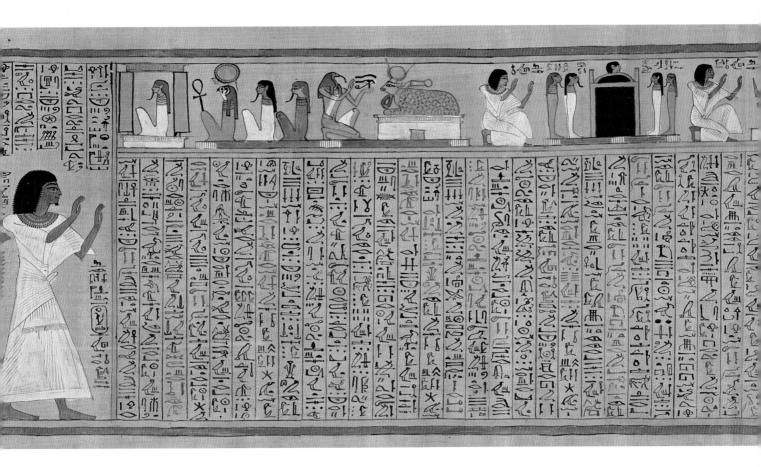

even by the ancient Egyptians.

Hunefer's copy of it is actually not very good, perhaps because it is so mysterious and difficult. The copyist missed out quite a few sentences, and garbled words in some places, especially towards the end. And the pictures don't line up with the right parts of the spell!

Hunefer's papyrus has a special extra picture in the middle of the spell. It shows Hunefer and Nasha worshipping the gods in the other pictures.

Above this extra picture, there is a prayer summing up Hunefer's hopes for a comfortable afterlife:

'Hail to you, lords of the West, you company of gods in the land of the dead! May they allow going in and coming out! I will not be turned back at the doors of the lords of the underworld! May I receive cakes from the altars of the lords of eternity! ... May I be given bread from the House of Bread, and cool water from the House of Cool Water!'

Later Hunefer says:

> 'I am a great one of the gods who help Horus, who speak about what their lord loves!'
> *'What does that mean?'*
> 'Imseti, Hapi, Duamutef, Qebehsenuf'

These are the names of the four sons of Horus who help him. They guard the organs removed in mummification, such as the stomach and the liver. These organs were placed in the tomb in four jars, each decorated with the head of one of these four gods.

In the picture, Hunefer worships the four gods who stand around a chest that contains the organs of Osiris Hunefer. His head rises up out of the top of the chest, showing that he is alive and reborn.

Four jars with the heads of the four gods.

And now Hunefer says mysteriously:

'I am the big cat that split the sacred tree beside him in the city of Iunu on that night of fighting ... on that day when the enemies of the Lord of All were destroyed.'
'What does that mean?'
'As for "the great cat", he is the Sun god himself, who was called "cat" because the god of cleverness spoke truly.'

Like many spells, this works through wordplay. The words for 'cat' and 'truly' sound very similar in ancient Egyptian: 'meu' and 'maau'. At the far right, the picture shows the Sun god as a wild cat killing his enemy, the serpent of darkness, beside the tree. Because Hunefer can recite this spell and knows about this myth, he will triumph over darkness and death like the divine cat.

This is the part of the spell about the big cat – quite a long way from the picture.

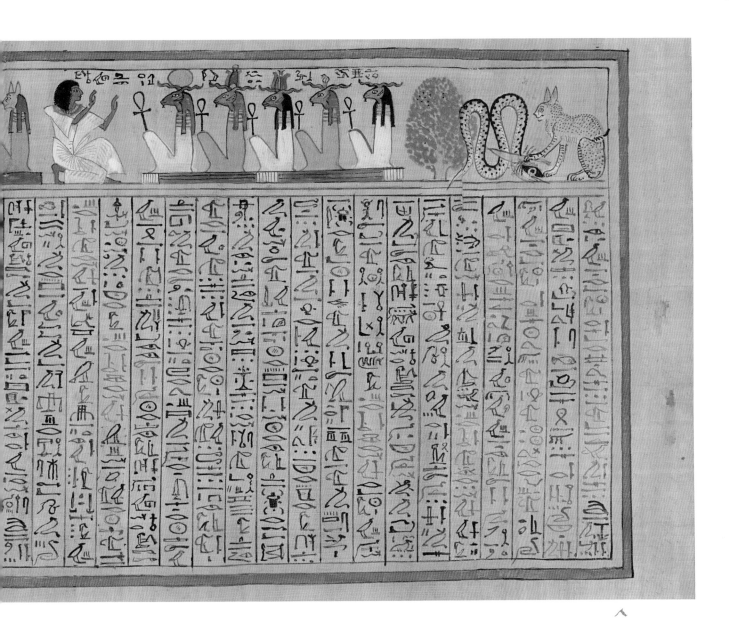

The book ends here with a final coloured border and another margin. The spell stops suddenly in mid-sentence at the bottom of the final line, nowhere near the end of the full spell. We don't know why the painter and copyist stopped here – perhaps they had to finish off this expensive book quickly and unexpectedly.

Missing spells

Hunefer's papyrus finishes suddenly, and it is only 5.5 metres long. This is very short compared to the papyrus of another scribe called Ani, which is almost 24 metres!

Hunefer's book could have included many other spells, like Ani's. These pictures come from Ani's papyrus.

'Spell for entering the hidden portals of the House of Osiris'

Other spells include: 'spell for avoiding traps', 'spell for not letting the corpse rot' and 'spell for not eating excrement or drinking urine'.

'Spell for changing into a snake'

'Spell for changing into a heron'

One of the spells in the Book of the Dead collection has a picture-map of the 'Field of Reeds'. This is a paradise of green fields and canals, just like the fertile land of Egypt beside the Nile. Here the dead could enjoy an eternal life with family and friends. This 'Field of Reeds' is painted on the wall of the tomb of an architect called Sennedjem. This lovely landscape was the goal of Hunefer's journey through the dangers of death.

What happened to the papyrus

Hunefer's mummy was buried in a small chamber cut into the hills behind the temple of his king Sety. The papyrus was placed inside a wooden statue of the god Osiris. This statue was put in the burial chamber and then the chamber was sealed and hidden.

The statue and papyrus were discovered some time in the nineteenth century. The papyrus was bought by a French doctor working for the Egyptian government, Antoine Clot (1793–1868). He collected many antiquities, and in 1852 he sold this papyrus to the British Museum. We don't know what happened to everything else from Hunefer's tomb.

Hunefer's name is painted on the front of this small wooden statue of the mummified god. There is a secret compartment in the back of the statue for the papyrus roll.

A museum conservator, Bridget Leach, studying the paints on the papyrus.

When the papyrus was discovered in Hunefer's tomb, it had not decayed at all. When it arrived in the Museum, it was cut into sections and these were placed in glass frames to protect them. Some of the paints and even the papyrus itself fade in the light, and so the Museum now keeps the papyrus in a special dark storeroom.

Even today, the papyrus with Hunefer's name keeps his name and memory alive, and we still see him and his wife calmly confronting the old enemy, death.

'Thoth has made the sunlight shine upon your chest! He lights up for you the way of darkness! He drives any evil away from your body by the power of his spells!'

Find out more

M. Hooper, *The Tomb of Nebamun: Explore an Ancient Egyptian Tomb.*
London: British Museum Press 2008.

R. B. Parkinson, *Pocket Guide to Ancient Egyptian Hieroglyphs.*
London: British Museum Press; New York: Barnes and Noble 2003.

R. Parkinson, *The Complete Book of the Dead of Hunefer: A Pullout Papyrus.*
London: British Museum Press 2010.

C. Thorne, *Draw Like an Egyptian.* London: British Museum Press 2007.

For older readers:

B. J. Kemp, *How to Read the Egyptian Book of the Dead.* London:
Granta Books 2007.

J. H. Taylor (ed.), *Journey through the Afterlife: Ancient Egyptian Book of the Dead.*
London: British Museum Press 2010.

J. H. Taylor, *Spells for Eternity: The Ancient Egyptian Book of the Dead.*
London: British Museum Press 2010.

Translation of all the spells: R. O. Faulkner, *The Ancient Egyptian Book of the Dead.*
London: British Museum Press 2010 (latest edn).

Overleaf: This is the landscape of the Nile Valley,
which Hunefer wanted to live in forever.